creepy creatures

Published by Creative Paperbacks
P.O. Box 227, Mankato, Minnesota 56002
Creative Paperbacks is an imprint of
The Creative Company
www.thecreativecompany.us

Design and production by Ellen Huber
Art direction by Rita Marshall
Printed in the United States of America

Photographs by 123rf (Adrian Hillman), CanStock
(Antrey, Dreamframer, magraphics, peresanz,
stana, Vaida_P), Dreamstime (Amwu, Dashark,
Isselee, Orionmystery, Stocksnapper, Unteroffizier,
Vladvitek), Getty Images (Michael Durham, Mark
Moffett, Piotr Naskrecki), iStockphoto (Antagain,
arlindo71, Evgeniy Ayupov, Eric Isselée, spxChrome,
TommyIX), Shutterstock (discpicture, Henrik
Larsson, Peter Waters, Pan Xunbin), SuperStock
(Belinda Images, Minden Pictures), Veer (defun,
japape, rufar)

Library of Congress Cataloging-in-Publication Data
Bodden, Valerie.
Ants / by Valerie Bodden.
p. cm. — (Creepy creatures)
Summary: A basic introduction to ants, examining
where they live, how they grow, what they eat, and
the unique traits that help to define them, such as
their tirelessly hardworking behavior.
Includes bibliographical references and index.
ISBN 978-1-60818-230-5 (hardcover)
ISBN 978-0-89812-793-5 (pbk)
1. Ants—Juvenile literature. I. Title.
QL568.F7B575 2013
595.79'6—dc23   2011050282

First Edition
9 8 7 6 5 4 3 2 1

CONTENTS

Introduction 4

What Is an Ant? 7

An Ant's Life 13

Make an Anthill 22

Glossary 23

Read More 24

Web Sites 24

Index 24

ants

VALERIE BODDEN

CRE A TIVE
PAPER BACKS

You are having a picnic outside.
You see something crawling across
the table. You take a closer look.

It is an ant!

An ant's legs are attached to a body part called the thorax

Ants are insects. They have three body parts and six legs. Ants have two **antennae** (*an-TEH-nee*). They have strong jaws. Some kinds of ants have stingers.

Ants carry food such as leaves in their jaws

Many weaver ants are green and live in trees

Most ants are black,
brown, yellow, or red.
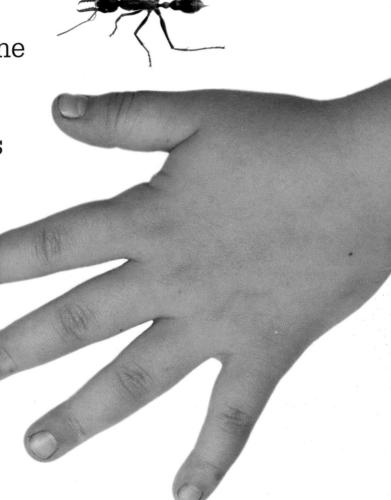
The smallest ants are the
size of a grain of sand.
The biggest ants are as
long as your thumb!

There are about 15,000 kinds of ants. Big black ants called carpenter ants are common in the United States and Canada.

Red imported fire ants come from South America

Red imported fire ants live in the southern U.S. They can sting people.

Ants live almost everywhere on Earth. But they do not live in the coldest places or in water. Most ants make nests underground or in trees. Ants have to watch out for **predators**. Spiders, lizards, birds, anteaters, and bears all eat ants.

Ants can be food for a spider, lizard, or anteater

Ants begin their lives in eggs. A **larva** comes out of each egg. The larva looks like a fat, white worm. The larva becomes a **pupa**. The pupa might have a silk covering called a cocoon around it. The pupa changes into an adult. Most adult ants live a few months.

Ants called workers watch over the larvae

Ants like to eat nectar from flowers before the flowers open

Many ants eat a sweet liquid called nectar from flowers. Others eat seeds, grass, berries, other parts of plants, or **fungus**. Some ants eat honeydew. This is a liquid made by insects called aphids (*A-fidz*). Some kinds of ants eat insects, caterpillars, and even lizards!

Ants work together to move large food such as mushrooms

Ants live in big groups called colonies. Ant colonies can have millions of ants! Each colony has one queen that lays eggs. Worker ants take care of the colony. All worker ants are female. Male ants have wings. They join special winged females to start new colonies.

After a winged female lays eggs, she loses her wings

Some army ants attack as a swarm to get food

People in some parts of the world eat ants.
There are many stories about ants, too.
People say that ants are hard workers.
Some people keep ant farms so they can
watch ants dig tunnels.
It can be fun finding
and watching these
busy creepy creatures!

Ant farms are usually see-through and shaped as a box

MAKE AN ANTHILL

Many kinds of ants make nests underground. The top of the nest often looks like a small hill of sand. You can make your own anthill. First, draw a hill shape on a piece of paper. Cut out the hill. Then, spread glue all over it. Pour some sand over the glue. Let the glue dry. Use black paint to make some ants on your anthill!

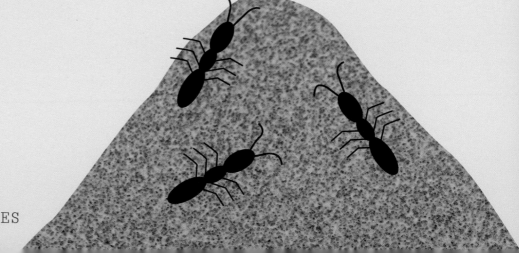

GLOSSARY

antennae: feelers on the heads of some insects that are used to touch, smell, and taste things

fungus: a plantlike living thing that has no roots or leaves; it grows on other living things or on dead or rotting plants

larva: the form some insects and animals take when they hatch from eggs, before changing into their adult form

predators: animals that kill and eat other animals

pupa: an insect that is changing from a larva into an adult, usually while inside a covering or case to keep it safe

READ MORE

Green, Emily K. *Ants*. Minneapolis: Bellwether Media, 2007.

Kalz, Jill. *Ant Colonies*. North Mankato, Minn.: Smart Apple Media, 2002.

WEB SITES

Enchanted Learning: Ants
http://www.enchantedlearning.com/subjects/insects/ant/Antcoloringpage.shtml
Learn more about ants, and print out an ant picture to color.

Natural History Museum: Antcam
http://www.nhm.ac.uk/kids-only/naturecams/antcam/
Watch a huge colony of ants crawling around.

INDEX

antennae 7

colonies 18

colors 9

eggs 14, 18

foods 17

homes 13, 22

kinds 10, 11

larvae 14

life span 14

predators 13

pupae 14

queens 18

sizes 9

workers 19